The Lie Detector

Susan Gates

Illustrated by Ivan Bates

OXFORD
UNIVERSITY PRESS

D0232195

Chapter 1

There's one thing wrong with Gemma, my best friend. She tells a lot of lies. And it's really stupid because we all know that they're not true.

For instance, yesterday she said, 'My mum's got me some new trainers. You know, the really expensive ones, like you've got.

'Only mine have got purple flashes down the side, not pink ones.'

So I said, 'Where are these new shoes then? Why don't you wear them to school?'

I wear my expensive new trainers all the time.

Gemma said, 'I'm not going to wear them for school. They'll get spoiled. I'm keeping them for best.'

Of course I knew she
hadn't got any new shoes.
Just like she hasn't
got her own TV
in her room...

...or her own computer
or any of the other
things she's always
boasting about.

I mean, I've been to her house.
They've only got one TV and they
haven't got a computer at all. So why
does she bother lying?

When I got my own video for my bedroom, guess what Gemma did?

You're right! About two days later she came up to me and said, 'I've got a video in my bedroom too!'

I thought, 'This time she's not getting away with it!' I mean, I hate boasting, don't you? So I said, quick as a flash, 'Let's go and watch a film on it then! Let's watch the new Disney film again.'

I've got loads of videos of my own. Whenever I want one, my mum buys it for me. You should see them! I've got shelves and shelves full of them.

Gemma looked all confused, just like I knew she would, and said, 'We can't watch a video today.'

'Oh, why not?' I said in my most sarcastic voice.

'Well,' Gemma said, 'my video machine's gone to be mended.'

'I thought you just said it was brand new? I thought you said you just got it?'

'Well, I did, but I spilt some orange juice in it and smoke came out and it had to go back to the shop!'

Chapter 2

So that's what my friend Gemma's
like. I mean, she's my best friend and I
really like her, but I'm getting pretty
fed up of all those lies. They're not
even good lies either. They're pathetic.
For instance, my mum buys me lots of
new clothes. She buys me whatever I
want. And I always wear my new
clothes to school to show everyone.

Every time I get new clothes Gemma says something like, 'My mum bought me some lovely black silky trousers yesterday. Just like the ones you've got.'

So why doesn't she wear them to school? Why does she always turn up in old hand-me-down stuff from her big sister? Why does she say, 'I'm keeping my new trousers for best. I don't want to spoil them'?

I'll give you one guess. You're right! Because she hasn't got any new trousers, that's why. She hasn't got any of the new things she says she has.

As you can imagine, Gemma's lies are really getting on my nerves. Well, I bet you'd feel the same, wouldn't you?

So, I've had this brilliant idea. I've decided to teach Gemma a lesson. It's for her own good. She just makes herself look silly telling all those lies, when everyone knows all along that they aren't true.

I've invented a lie detector.

Yes, honestly! It's not a real lie detector of course, but I'm going to tell Gemma it is.

I made it from the electronics kit I got for my birthday. It was easy to make. And it looks really good, you should see it.

It's got a little red light bulb and a little green light bulb and they're on a piece of wood.

I followed the instructions and wired them up to a torch battery. Then I fixed two secret switches underneath, so I can turn on the lights without anyone knowing.

The red light is for truth.

The green light is for lies. That's because my Gran always says, 'I can tell you're lying, because your eyes go green.' Which is a silly thing to say because my eyes are green anyway!

Chapter 3

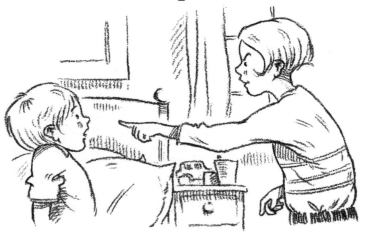

Last night I tried out my invention.

I tried it out on my brother. It
worked like a dream. I went into his
bedroom with the lie detector in my
pocket and I said, 'Now, tell me the
truth, did you take my coloured
pencils out of my bedroom?'

Of course I knew that he had
because I'd just seen them, poking out
from under his pillow.

'No, of course I didn't. Why are you blaming me?' my brother said, looking innocent.

I whipped my lie detector from my pocket and secretly pressed the green light.

'What's that?' asked my brother.

'It's a lie detector,' I told him in a stern voice. 'And if you tell a lie, the green light flashes. And if you tell the truth, the red light goes on.'

'Come on, you're joking,' he said.
But he looked a bit worried.

'OK, I'll prove it to you,' I said. 'Did
your new school tie *really* get cut in
half by accident?'

'Of course!' said my brother. 'It
happened just like I told Mum. It got
trapped in a door!'

But I knew it hadn't, because I saw him cutting it in half with scissors. So I pressed the green light.

'The lie detector always knows,' I said in a spooky voice. 'It can read your mind.'

'I didn't do it. It wasn't my fault,' said my brother.

I pressed the green light again.

'Tell the truth!'

'OK, OK,' said my brother. 'I cut my tie in half. All right? It was too long. It went down to my knees!'

Secretly, I pressed the red light.

'See?' I said. 'The lie detector always knows when you tell the truth. Now tell me if you took those pencils!'

'No, I didn't, honest.'

Flash, flash went the green light.

'OK, OK, I confess!' said my brother. 'It was me.' And he got my pencils from under his pillow.

Then he said, 'Give me that lie detector!' He held out his hand. 'I want to ask *you* some questions now. I want to see if *you* tell the truth!'

'No,' I said quickly, hiding the lie detector behind my back. 'I'm not going to give it to you. You might break it. But you can ask me some questions if you like. And the lie detector will show if I'm telling the truth or not.'

'Did you eat the last chocolate yoghurt?' asked my brother. 'The one I was saving for myself?'

'No, I didn't!' I said angrily.

'I'll bet you did!' said my brother. 'What does the lie detector say?'

I held out the lie detector. And guess what? You're right. The red button flashed.

'See?' I said. 'That proves I'm telling the truth.'

My brother looked puzzled. 'I was sure that you ate it!'

'Well, I didn't! So don't blame me.'

'Where did you get that lie detector thing?' asked my brother.

'Ah ha,' I said, tapping the side of my nose. 'Wouldn't you like to know?'

'I don't like it,' he said. 'It's creepy having something that can read your mind like that.'

Chapter 4

I don't think my lie detector's creepy.
I think it's great. I think it's a brilliant
invention!

My brother thought it was real and
he's quite brainy. So I bet I won't have
any trouble making Gemma believe in
it too.

Anyway, it's in my coat pocket now.
I'm just waiting for Gemma to come
into the playground and I'm going to
try it out on her.

While I'm waiting for Gemma, I play a little game with the lie detector. I take it out and say to it, 'OK, lie detector, I really didn't take that last chocolate yoghurt. Cross my heart and hope to die. I'm telling the truth, aren't I?'

If it was a real lie detector the green light should light up. Because I did eat the last chocolate yoghurt. Well, I didn't know my brother wanted it for himself, did I?

But it's only a pretend lie detector. And *I'm* pressing the buttons. So the lie detector has to do what I say.

I press the red button. Flash, flash, flash.

'Tee hee!' I'm grinning like mad. 'I
was telling the truth. The lie detector
says so!'

Here comes Gemma. I hide the lie
detector in my pocket.

I know she's going to start lying
straight away because two days ago I
got a new pair of roller boots. Of
course I couldn't wear them in school.
But I brought them to show everyone.
They're white and silver with silver
laces. All the girls said they wanted a
pair just like them.

What did I tell you?

Gemma waves at me and the first thing she says is, 'I've got a pair of roller boots just like the ones you brought to school. Except mine have got golden laces.'

It's lie detector time! I whip it out of my coat pocket. 'Say that again, Gemma.'

Chapter 5

Gemma looks confused. She looks at
my lie detector. 'What's that?' she says.

'It's a lie detector.' I tell her all about
the red light for truth and the green
light for lies. By now a crowd is
gathering round us.

'Where did you get it from?' Gemma
wants to know.

'Never mind where I got it from.
Just say that again about the roller
boots and I'll show you how it works.'

Gemma looks worried. But she says
slowly, 'I've got a pair of roller boots,
just like yours. Except mine have got
golden laces.'

Secretly, I switch on the green light.

'There you are. I told you. The green light's flashing. That means Gemma's lying!' I tell the crowd around us.

'I'm not, I'm not lying,' says Gemma.

'All right then, let's try another question. Have you got your own TV in your bedroom like you said?'

'Yes,' says Gemma. But she says it in a small, quiet voice.

I make the green light flash on and off. 'It's no good lying,' I tell her. 'This lie detector can read your mind.'

I make the green light flash again.

'No,' says Gemma, 'I haven't got a TV in my bedroom.'

'Ah ha! The truth at last,' I say and press the red light.

It's a great invention, this lie detector! You can't tell it isn't a real one!

But what's that, sparkling in Gemma's eye? Is that a tear?

I can't believe it. What's she crying for? I'm only having a little game. I'm only teaching her a little lesson, to stop her telling lies.

Then Gemma says, before I've even asked her, 'And I haven't got a video either. Or new trousers or any of the things you've got. I know I shouldn't have said I'd got them. But I just couldn't help it.'

I thought the crowd around us would clap or something. I thought they'd say, 'That lie detector's brilliant! Where can we get one?'

But they don't. They've gone all quiet. What's the matter with them?

Gemma is wiping her eyes on the sleeve of her coat.

Chapter 6

Suddenly I feel awful. Everyone's staring at me like I've done something wrong and Gemma can't stop crying. I didn't mean her to cry like that. Honest I didn't. It was just a game.

'Look,' I tell Gemma. 'It wasn't my fault. I didn't say you were telling lies. It wasn't anything to do with me. It was the lie detector!'

The green light on the lie detector starts flashing.

Why is it doing that? I'm not pressing it! Honestly I'm not. It's really bright. It lights up all our faces. A weedy little torch battery can't make it glow like that!

I try to press the red light. But it makes no difference!

It's scary, creepy. I don't like what's happening. I say to Gemma, 'Look, we're still best friends, aren't we?'

'Yes,' says Gemma.

But when she says it, the green light flashes even brighter.

'It's no good,' sighs Gemma, watching the green light. 'The lie detector knows I'm lying. The truth is I don't want you as a best friend any more. You're a horrible best friend!'

I can't believe it!

'No, I'm not!' I shout. 'I'm not a horrible friend!' The green light flashes on and on and on. I'm pressing the secret switches. But I can't make it stop.

'See,' says Gemma. 'The lie detector knows the truth.'

Then someone in the crowd says, 'You're always picking on Gemma. You make her feel bad because she hasn't got new clothes and things.'

'And you're always boasting about all the things you've got,' says someone else.

'No, I'm not!' I cry. What's happening? This is all going wrong. The lie detector is supposed to do what I say. It's supposed to be teaching Gemma a lesson! I try the red switch again but it won't work and the lie detector dazzles us with its brilliant green flashes.

Chapter 7

'I wish I'd never made this lie detector!' I tell everyone. 'I'm really sorry that I made it!'

An amazing thing happens. At last, the green light goes off. The red light flashes.

'I'm really sorry, Gemma,' I say.

The red light glows like fire.

'So can we still be friends? I won't say nasty things about your clothes. I won't keep boasting about all my new things. I'll try not to. I mean it.'

For a second I'm really scared that the green light will glow again. But it doesn't. The red light stays on.

'See, she is telling the truth, Gemma,' says someone. 'The lie detector says so. She does mean it.'

'Please, Gemma,' I say.

Gemma's thinking about it. There's a long pause. Then she says, 'All right. We can still be best friends.'

And I'm really pleased. Because the lie detector doesn't go green this time. The brilliant red light shines on and on and on.

I've decided. I'm going to throw that lie detector away. My dad said it was probably a loose wire or something that made those lights flash off and on by themselves. He says I could easily mend it.

But I'm not so sure. I'm going to throw it away. It's far too dangerous to have around. Unless *you* want it, of course? You can have it if you want to. Only don't blame me if it starts telling you the truth!

About the author

My mother used to say, 'Susan, it's easy to tell when you're lying because your eyes always go so green!'

Now I live in County Durham with three children of my own. And, sometimes, when they all blame each other, I'd love to have an easy way to tell who is lying and who isn't. My son said, 'You need a lie detector, Mum. That would solve all your problems.' I said, 'What a good idea.' But then I began to think about it. And I decided that a lie detector might cause more problems than it solved!